HOCKEY JUST FOR MOMS

AND ANYONE ELSE THAT'S INTERESTED

Where did it start and what's it all about

Written by: R. Benjamin Jordan

Illustrated by: Elissa Quist

Copyright August 2016 under the title "Hockey Just for Moms – And Anyone Else That's Interested" by R. Benjamin Jordan (a.k.a. Coach Grampa) owner, author, and publisher.

All rights reserved. No part of this publication may be reproduced, transmitted, transcribed, stored in a retrieval system, or translated into any language in any form by any means without the written permission of the owner.

Table of Contents

Foreward		4
Dedication		6
Introduction		7
Chapter 1	What's it All About	10
Chapter 2	The Rink	15
Chapter 3	The Players	18
Chapter 4	The Offense and Defense	25
Chapter 5	The Play	27
Chapter 6	The Rules	31
Chapter 7	The Game	48
Glossary		52
One last Thing		59

FOREWARD

Foreword by Lisa Cohn, an award-winning writer and author whose articles about youth sports have appeared in the Christian Science Monitor, Yahoo! Parenting, Huffington Post and other publications. She played soccer, lacrosse, and ice hockey at Wesleyan University. Lisa is a co-founder of www.YouthSportsPsychology.com and www.KidsSportsPsychology.com.

In the 1960s, youth football coach R. "Bob" Benjamin Jordan (a.k.a. Coach Grampa) was concerned with some of the dads coaching from the sidelines.

"Several of the dads had strong opinions that were sometimes different from the coaches," he recalls. They were vocal so, "I devised a plan to win the dads over through the moms. The moms were the glue that held the team together. They brought snacks for halftime, provided transportation, kept dinner warm, and washed dirty uniforms."

His plan: to teach moms how to play football so they could better understand what the kids were experiencing and could use that understanding to influence the fathers.

"We had the first session in my basement. I showed the moms about equipment, and how to wear it. Then we moved to the field. We ran plays, ran defense and worked on kicking. The moms did everything their kids would do, except knock each other down"

Of course, all along Jordan's aim was to build the confidence of the kids on his team. He thought that the players' confidence was affected by the way some dads behaved. "Every kid has something he does well and it takes time to find it, but the dads wanted it to happen too fast. The kids would get discouraged and feel as if they couldn't live up to their fathers' expectations," he said.

As a result of Jordan's experiment, the moms served as assistant coaches because they understood the game and what the kids were going through. The moms were better able to communicate to the fathers how they should behave on the sidelines.

As for the kids, they loved the fact that their mothers played football and understood the game.

Now, Jordan is taking his wisdom to moms in a bigger way, with his series of books for mothers (and anyone else who is interested) about sports. In addition to giving tips, he provides some history about how each particular sport originated and evolved--information that can help moms and dads put sports in context for their kids and help them enjoy sports more. With 35 years of coaching experience behind him, and a sincere desire to improve the youth sports scene, Jordan has a unique take on how to make sports more enjoyable for kids.

--Lisa Cohn

Dedication

This book is dedicated to the mothers of little league, elementary school, middle school, and high school athletes everywhere. Without your dedication, support, and labors, youth sports would not be complete. Thank you. You deserve recognition, and our appreciation.

NOTE: This book is intended for mothers of athletes and anyone else that's interested; the content is directed at the beginning levels and up to and including high school. There is no discussion of the college or professional levels. If any others, besides mothers, wish to read this book feel free to do so with the author's gratitude.

Also a giant thank you to Mimi, Nancye, Lynn, Kristine, and Elissa all mothers of athletes.

Other sports books by R. Benjamin Jordan (a.k.a. Coach Grampa)
    Origin and Evolution of American Football
    Football Just for Moms – And Anyone Else That's Interested
    Soccer Just for Moms – And Anyone Else That's Interested

Coming in the winter of 2016/2017
    Lacrosse Just for Moms – And Anyone Else That's Interested
    Volleyball Just for Moms – And Anyone Else That's Interested

Introduction

The origin of ice hockey is mysterious, there is no definitive year, month, day, or time it began; it is believed to be one of the earliest sports in the world. It wasn't until the 1800's that ice hockey started to come into its own and found its place in the world of sports.

Stick-and ball-games may be as old as civilization and they may have originated in Persia, Egypt, or China, but no one knows for sure. There is archaeological evidence of ball-and-stick games being played in Greece in the 400's BCE.

A sport that is like hockey was being played during the first millennium BC in Ireland; it was called "hurling." During the Middle Ages (5th to 15th centuries) there were a number of similar sports played in Europe. In Scotland it was "shinty," in England there was "bandy ball." The Norse had been playing "knattleikr" for a thousand years or more. Most all of these games were played on land, but in the winter months they were played on frozen ponds, lakes, and rivers. There are numerous accounts of games being played on frozen bodies of water in the 1600's and 1700's in Ireland, England, Scotland as well as the Scandinavian countries.

Hockey, as we know it today, had its beginnings in Canada in the 1800's. The most accepted story is that the boys at King's College School (Canada's first college established in 1788) in Windsor, Nova Scotia adapted the field game of Hurley to ice on the local ponds and originated a new winter game – Ice Hurley, which evolved into Ice Hockey. The British soldiers stationed in Canada took up the game and were the main reason it spread. As they were reassigned they took the game with them and it slowly moved west.

In 1872 a young man from Halifax, Nova Scotia named James Creighton moved to Montreal and with him he brought *Ice Hockey* and the first rules, known as the Halifax Rules. After involving a number of his friends, he organized a group of players to practice and learn indoors at the Victoria Skating Rink. In 1875

Creighton presented an exhibition of the game which is generally recognized as the first indoor ice hockey game.

The early games were played with a ball rather than a puck. The ball lost favor because it broke too many windows when it moved indoors. Some earlier games were played with a wooden disc, or a "bung" (a plug of cork or oak used to plug a barrel). Today's pucks are made of vulcanized rubber.

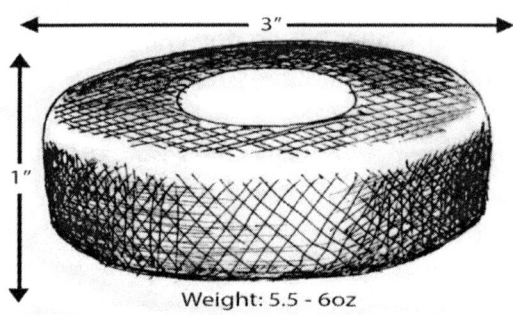
Weight: 5.5 - 6oz

There is some controversy over the origin of the name "puck." Some say it is related to the verb puck for striking or pushing the ball, or from the Scottish Gaelic *puc* or the Irish *poc*, meaning to poke, punch, or deliver a blow. Early sticks were made from the branches of willow trees. The Mi'kmaq, a First Nations people of Nova Scotia, were playing ice hockey in the 18th Century and in the 19th Century; they are credited with developing the "hockey stick," carved from sugar maple wood.

The French word "hoquet" (shepherd's crook) is generally believed to be the origin of the name "hockey." Although the name was given to the game in the 18th Century, it wasn't in common use until the 19th Century.

Ice hockey came to the United States by British soldiers and immigrants. The first game in the U.S. was in 1893. It has been a slow growth, but today it's enjoying a rapid increase in popularity, especially at the younger ages, and high school.

Ice hockey has had its darker period because of extreme violence. In 1905 a hockey player was put on trial for killing an opposing player with a blow. In 1907 another player was indicted for the same reason. Both players were found innocent, but the country called for legislation to curb the violence.

USA Hockey, whose main focus is youth hockey, was founded on October 29, 1937. It began as the Amateur Hockey Association of the United States (AHAUS), but changed its name to the present USA Hockey in 1991. They are based in Colorado Springs, Colorado. USA Hockey is the recognized governing body for amateur hockey in the United States, and currently have over one million members. On their web site usahockey.com they offer a handbook for hockey parents, which I highly recommend you obtain. It is informational, as well as entertaining. A must read for hockey parents, especially parents of new hockey players. USA Hockey establishes the various age groups and identifications described in Chapter 3 The Players.

What do I do now?

Chapter 1 – What's it all About

Hockey is a simple game and is best described as a contact sport played on ice, usually in a rink, in which two teams of skaters use their sticks to shoot a vulcanized rubber puck into their opponent's net to score points. Ice hockey usually consists of six players each; one a goaltender, and five players who skate up and down the ice trying to take the puck and score a goal against the opposing team. Hockey is a continuous action sport.

Like all sports, especially at the beginning level and the learning stages, there is the game and THE GAME. The game is the sport of hockey. It is the learning of individual and team techniques, the development of skills, the practice sessions, the teamwork required, the sportsmanship, the friendship, and the rules. THE GAME is the grand and glorious occasion when two opposing groups of players, who have been working hard to learn the game, have the opportunity to display their skills in open competition against an opposing team. It is not a matter of life or death, it's a game.

The game and THE GAME are inseparable. You cannot have one without the other. Players cannot participate in THE GAME until they learn the game. Even though the game and THE GAME are inseparable, there should be different degrees of importance placed on them within the levels of competition.

At the beginning levels - generally youth leagues or elementary school – the heavy emphasis should be on the game. Young players require a great deal of teaching in the correct individual skills and techniques of hockey. The rules, objectives, and terminologies of hockey may not be clear to them in the beginning.

A strong commitment by a coach or parent to teaching the game will allow young players to learn and develop to their individual levels without destroying their confidence, or their interest in hockey. All youngsters learn and develop at different paces. Some are quick to learn, while others take more time. Every young player has some specific physical or mental talent that exceeds his/her other abilities. For example a youngster may be a fast skater, or have a knack for handling the stick. Some have a natural understanding of the game, and some may be good at defending the goal. The point is that all young players have something they do well. When they first begin participating in hockey, the good coach will find that dominant talent and build on it.

An overemphasis on THE GAME at the beginning levels of competition is a major criticism for young people playing sports at an early age. Being "Number 1" can easily become the primary objective of overzealous adults. Elaborate team tryouts, pre-arranged team membership, league standings, trophies, and championships can too often distort the important goals and objectives of athletic competition for young athletes.

As the players progress to the higher levels of competition the emphasis on THE GAME should become stronger. However, the individual's learning and development should never be sacrificed for the sake of THE GAME. Winning THE GAME should not be the only acceptable result from a player's efforts.

Much has been written and said about youth sports and it has many critics who say they are cruel, dehumanizing, and damaging to young people, both physically and emotionally. The defenders say they build character, teach responsibility, create confidence, promote teamwork, and enhance physical skills. The truth is that youth sports do neither. The responsibility for a player being helped or harmed lies directly with the adults who coach, officiate, administer, and parent the player. Remember, all sports are an athletic competition and entertainment. The adult's approach, attitude, and emphasis will ultimately determine whether a young player will suffer a negative experience, or enjoy a positive one.

One aspect of hockey that differentiates it from some other sports is it's a continuous action sport. There are no set plays as in football, or deliberate play as in baseball. It shares this feature with soccer, and lacrosse, and in some ways with basketball. Physical contact between players at the lower levels of competition is generally either accidental or unintentional, but is still against the rules. Physical contact is not taught and practiced.

Being a continuous action sport a player may be required to switch from offense to defense, or defense to offense, in a split second. Your player's team may be in control of the puck and is skating towards the opponents' goal. His/her offensive skills are on full display when suddenly an opposing player steals the puck and heads towards your goal; bang, your player now must display his/her defensive skills.

The skill most important to playing hockey is skating. Some young people pick up the skill of ice skating very quickly. It's relatively easy to skate in a forward direction by pushing one foot ahead of the other. In hockey that's essential, but it's not nearly enough. During THE GAME skaters are going full out, top speed; then all of a sudden they need to change direction, or skate backwards. Honing skating skills to handle all the offensive and defensive situations takes time for the beginning age groups. At all levels a great deal of practice time should be devoted to learning how to skate, and for the older levels, polishing and improving all their skills.

Hockey skates are different than regular ice skates or figure skating skates. The hockey skate boots are made from a combination of synthetic leather and hard ballistic nylon; they reach just above the ankle, and have a cushioned interior.

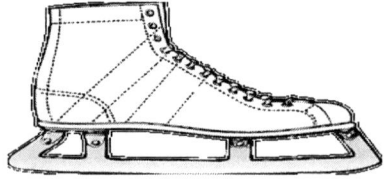

The blades are narrower than the other types of skates, and they have a more pronounced curve at the front and back and are flatter in the middle. Hockey skates are built for speed and stopping ability.

It is difficult to learn all the skills required to play hockey, such as skating fast, changing direction while handling a stick, and they are not mastered quickly. As skills develop, confidence increases. Being able to learn and master the physical aspects of hockey should be a growing and maturing process for young players.

Practice, Practice, Practice

     A young player's physical abilities and mental attitude change as they progress through the various levels of competition. Some may decide they don't like hockey and give it up, and that's okay – at least they tried. The only true failure is not trying. If a player wants to quit hockey I recommend they finish the season and not sign up the following year. It's important to learn to finish what you start.

     If you've already had a hockey player living in your home you are undoubtedly aware of the emotional extremes he/she can experience, from total depression to complete exhilaration. Those emotions come from the competition involved and the success, or non-success achieved. There are two types of competition in all team sports. One type is the competition with others, such as competing for a starting position with a teammate. The other type is the competition with yourself to perform better today than you did yesterday. Both types are healthy and important, but the emphasis (there's that word again) can get distorted. Adult encouragement is far more valuable than criticism for not winning the skating race, or the stick handling drill, during practice. Young players need massive doses of encouragement. Your player will experience success as well as failure, and both are acceptable. No one always succeeds, nor do they always fail. If the only lesson your hockey player learns is to deal with success and failure from difficult situations, that lesson alone will be valuable. Remember that the only true failure is not trying.

Playing on a team may be the young player's first experience with relying on others, or having others relying on him/her. Hockey is a team sport and it depends heavily on individuals performing tasks for the benefit of others. This teamwork and reliance on others could be one of the more valid lessons learned. All players receive some benefit from being on a hockey team, whether it is a beginning youth league team or a high school state champion. The camaraderie, the friendships, the heartache, the jubilation, the belonging, the competition, the satisfaction, the disappointments, the praise, and the sharing are all valuable assets that last a player a lifetime. Hockey should be a learning experience and it should be enjoyable, but most of all it should be fun – it's a game!

As your player grows into adulthood they will become part of a team. It will be at their job, it will be in a family, it may be in an organization, or in a movement, but there will be team work needed, and by playing team sports they should be well prepared to know what that means.

Earlier in this chapter I exaggerated the difference between the game, and THE GAME. In the following chapters you will learn about the rink, the player positions, the play itself, and the rules. In those chapters I won't distinguish between the game and THE GAME because as you read on you will see that you really can't separate them, except with emphasis.

Chapter 2 – The Rink

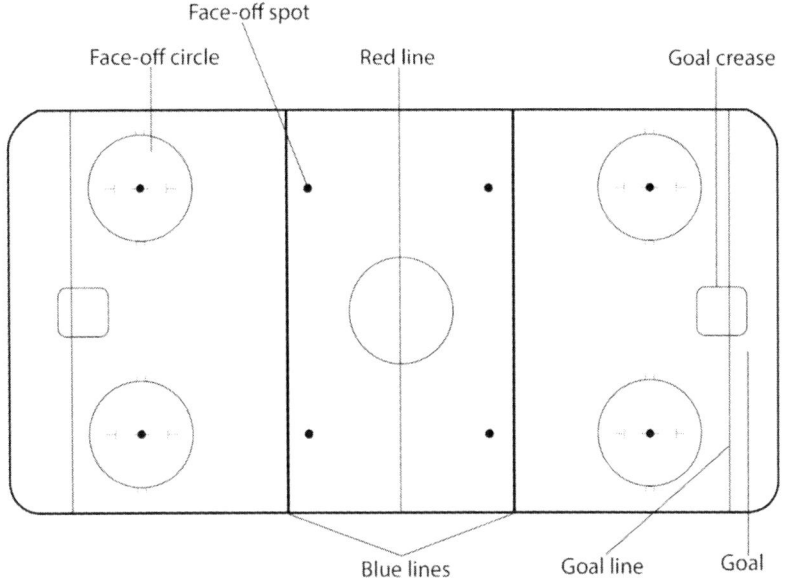

The ancient stick-and-ball games were wild affairs that were devoid of formal rules and regulations. Playing areas were any available frozen pond, river, or other body of water with shoveled off snow piled-up to act as boundaries. Just as the game has progressed and changed, so has the playing surface. As game rules and regulations were refined, the rink developed to accommodate the game. Today's hockey games are played on rinks of frozen ice that are precisely measured and marked to exact specifications.

The rink is a rectangular area 200 feet long by 85 feet wide, with rounded corners. Surrounding the playing surface are the *boards,* walls that measure from 40 inches to 48 inches high. The walls that line the sides of the rink are called *side boards* and the walls at the ends of the rink behind the goals are called *end boards.* Shatter proof glass walls are added to the sideboards and end boards to extend the height by another 5 feet. All of these walls and glass are to prevent the puck, which can travel upwards of 80 miles an hour by the older age groups, from flying into the spectators. The walls also keep players from doing likewise. See the above diagram for the names of the various lines, and areas.

The *goal line* is the "magic" line and the *net* the "promised land." In order to score a point a player must shoot the puck across the goal line and into the net. This is the only way to score in hockey and it's worth 1 point.

The playing surface is divided into 3 equal sections by use of 2 *blue lines.* The area between the 2 blue lines is called the *neutral zone.* The area between the blue lines and the goal are called the *attacking zone* or the *defending zone,* depending on which team is in control of the puck. A good way to tell the difference is that your team's defending zone is always to their backs, and they are facing the attacking zone. So, they attack what's in front of them and they defend what's in back of them. Remember that defending or attacking can change in a split second.

There is a red line running from sideboard to sideboard and is called the *center line.* This line is locate between the 2 blue lines and designates the halfway point between end boards. The two goal lines are also red in color and are located 12 feet from each end board.

There is a goal cage, more commonly known as the net, centered on each red goal line. This goal cage is made up of two upright bars connected by a crossbar. It is 4 feet high and 6 feet wide with nylon netting attached that extends 4 feet back. The goal cage is not anchored; it can be moved and the reason is safety. An anchored goal cage could cause an injury. If the goal cage does move play is stopped. There is a marked area just in front of the goal cage known as the *crease.* This is the goalie's free zone and no opposing player is allowed in the crease, or to interfere with the goalie.

There are a number of circles drawn on the ice. The circles are used by the *referees* or *linesmen* to start play after a stoppage.

On one side of the rink, behind the side boards are two areas where the players, not in the game, sit on benches along with *coaches, managers, and trainers.* On the opposite side of the rink behind the sideboards and in line with the red centerline, is an area for the *timekeepers,* and *official scorer;* there are also two *penalty boxes.* These boxes flank the area where the timekeeper and official scorer sit. The penalty boxes are for players who have committed an infraction to sit for a specified time as a penalty for committing the infraction.

All of these items will be discussed further in the Chapter 6 – The Play.

Chapter 3 – The Players

The total number of players on a team may vary depending on the level of competition, however only 6 players are allowed on the ice during a game The 6 are:

GOALIE – the goalie's responsibility is to stay near their goal and attempt to prevent shots from going into the net. The goalie gets in a position so that he/she can have a view of the action in front of him/her. The goalie wears more padding and larger equipment than the other players. All of a goalie's padding is thicker, and he/she uses 2 different types of gloves. The glove on the hand that holds the stick is padded and has a rectangular pad attached on the front

to help protect the back of his/her hand. The glove on the other hand is a large open glove used to catch or scoop up a puck. The glove on the stick hand is called a *blocking glove,* and the other one is called a *catching glove.* A goalie will wear a helmet with a mask attached, much like a baseball catcher's mask, and his/her skates are slightly different. The goalie's shin guards are large and heavily padded, and their stick is larger. All of the extra padding and larger equipment is to protect the goalie from the fast flying pucks being shot at the goal he/she is defending.

CENTER – the center is generally the leader of the team. He/she is responsible for directing the play both offensively and defensively. The center must be good at face-offs, be able to pass the puck, and shoot well. They are usually a very skilled skater and must lead on both ends of the ice. Since the center often possesses the puck he/she must be able to control the puck while he/she is moving towards the opponent's goal. Even though his/her position is in the center of the attack, he/she may be found anywhere on the ice. The center will also be called on to play defense if the possession suddenly changes.

WINGS – or wingers are positioned on each side of the center – a right wing and a left wing. Along with the center they make up the attacking line. The wings need to be excellent skaters and have good stick handling skills. They pass the puck to each other and to the center while trying to find the best shot at the goal. The left and right winger cover their respective sides, but like the center, may be found anywhere on the ice. The wings may also be called upon to suddenly play defense.

DEFENSEMEN – there are 2, one on the left and one on the right. They usually play to the rear of the attacking line with their backs to their goal, which, along with the goalie, they are responsible to defend. The left defends the left side, and the right is defended by the other one. They are also charged with harassing the opponent's respective wingers, and they can skate into the other areas on the ice. They are especially adept at skating backwards, and deflecting shots aimed at their goal. Even though their main responsibility is to defend, they may be found in the attacking zone.

Since hockey is a fast and furious continuous action sport all of the non-goalie positions may find themselves in all the areas of rink. They each have defined responsibilities on both offense and defense during the game, but circumstances may dictate they move around. Skating skills are put to the test for all 5 of the position players.

The non-goalie equipment worn by the other position players consists of shin guards covered by long socks, shoulder pads with rib protectors, elbow pads, pads to protect their hips, thighs and the area around the kidneys. They wear padded gloves with cuffs that overlap the elbow pads to protect the forearm. Lastly, all must wear padded helmets, and a protector for the face. To complete the equipment, they wear a team jersey, padded shorts (called breezers), long socks, and a mouth guard. Don't forget the tape, or Velcro – long socks tend to fall down so you need to use tape or Velcro around the tops to hold them up. You may find that wrapping is necessary, or a single layer – whatever works, use it.

Proper equipment is crucial. A young hockey player wears more equipment than any other sport. Most all hockey organizations have access to equipment retailers, some right in the building with the rink. Consult with them.

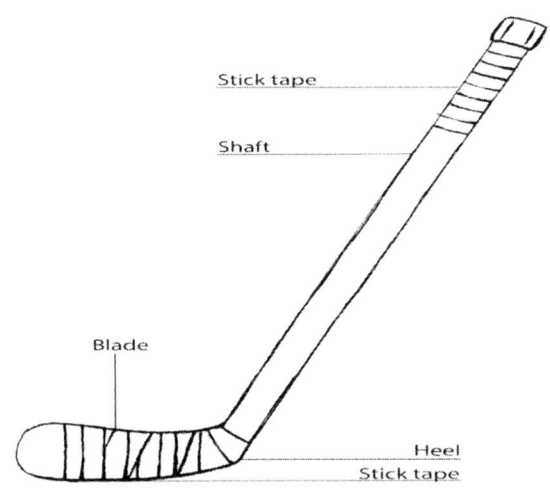

Typical hockey stick

They can advise on how to choose the stick, and what length it should be, properly fitting helmets, and skates. Let the experts sharpen the skates when needed. Even if you buy used equipment, get advice first. Once your player has experienced a year or two they will most probably outgrow their equipment and may need to upgrade. Always get advice from the people that know.

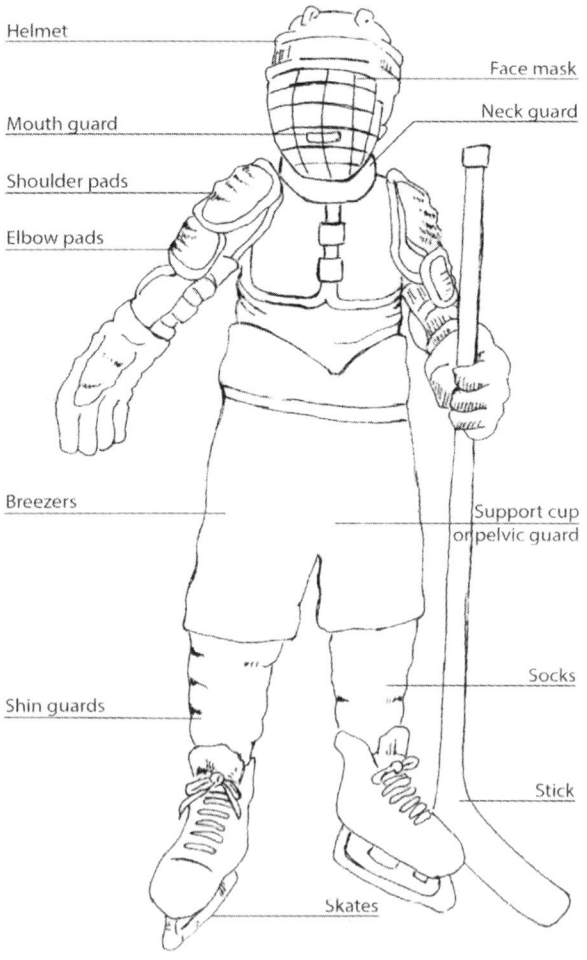

Before we leave the chapter on players, let me say a few words about how you can help your sons/daughters with their participation, especially the young ones. The two most important elements are sleep and nutrition. It's crucial they get enough rest, so make sure they get a good night's sleep. When it comes to nutrition, I bow to your wisdom and knowledge. You know what is good and bad for your child, even high school age when they lean towards "junk food." You are the expert here, not me. However, I insist you get your player a good strong water bottle to always take to practice and the games. You can put a distinctive marking on it so it's easy to find when needed. Keeping hydrated during practice and games is essential.

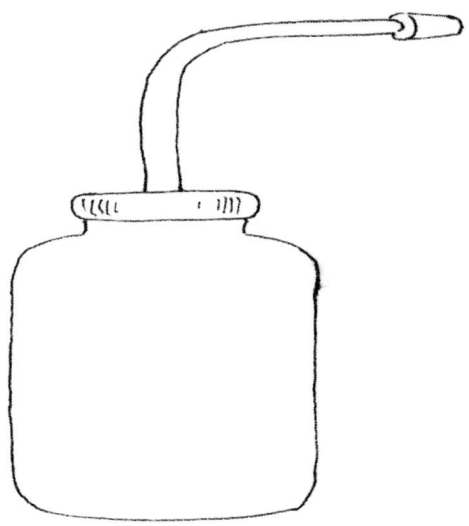

Go back to the Foreward and click on the two links there – a really good source for advice on being a sports parent, a very important element.

Since your players will most likely be in school during hockey season it poses the question of eligibility. In middle school and high school the school and the coaches determine if a player is academically eligible to play in the next game. When I coached, I left it up to the parents. If one of my players was not performing as they should in school the parent decided if they played in the next game. School should always come first, not sports.

Not all schools offer hockey so youth leagues have developed programs to cover ages from as young as 4 to as old as 18. These various levels are consistent throughout the country, but you should always check with your local organization. Generally the levels are:

Mini mites	4 years old to 7 years old
Mites	8 years old
Squirts	9 and 10 year olds
Peewee	11 and 12 year old
Bantam	13 and 14 years old
Midgets	15 to 18 years old

Within each of these levels there may be sub-levels based on experience and skill. They may be designated by A, AA, AAA, or some other type of identification. Lastly, I advise that you double check to make sure his/her equipment fits properly. With the little guys you moms are often responsible for getting them ready to go to practice. Learn about shoulder pads, and thigh pads, and helmets, etc. so that he/she is dressed properly and all the pads and such are in the correct place. There is nothing more uncomfortable than skates that are either too tight, or too loose.

No jewelry please; be sure your player doesn't wear their favorite ring, or necklace, or any other such item when they suit up. If there is any doubt, go to the coach for advice. Keep them healthy and safe with the proper fitting equipment. As they get older they should be able to suit up by themselves, and there will come a time with the older groups when parents are not allowed in the locker room.

Chapter 4 – The Offense and Defense

As stated earlier, hockey is a continuous action sport, so the action is non-stop and the switch from offense to defense can happen quickly, and vice versa.

Offense – when a player's stick is touching the puck and moving it he/she is in possession and his/her team is on offense, attacking the opponent's goal. The player in possession may pass the puck to a teammate, or shoot the puck at the goal. Players on offense may kick the puck, direct it with an open hand, or catch it and drop it. However the player may not use any of those actions to score a goal. Offensive players are facing the opponent's goal.

All offensive strategies have but one objective – score a goal. To do that they must advance the puck into the *attacking zone,* this is the area between the opposing blue line, and the goal. Teams have techniques for working together that they've practiced to get the puck into the attacking zone by advancing the puck one line at a time – first their blue line, then the center red line, and finally the opponent's blue line. A complication for the offensive efforts is the offside rule, which is explained in the chapter on rules. Offside in the younger age levels has spoiled many attacks.

Defense – defense in ice hockey is a very simple process. It is the act of preventing the offense from scoring a goal. The defending team's goalie plays the major role in the defense while the other 5 players create chaos in their attempts to steal the puck, disrupt the offensive play, and block or deflect shots on goal. In a word – the object of the defense is to prevent a score by the opposing team. Defensive players have their backs to their goal.

Defenders are taught to stay between the player with the puck, and their goalie. They can block shot attempts with his/her stick or his/her body. Defenders want to thwart the shot before it reaches the goalie.

Since ice hockey is a continuous action sport the action is stopped only in certain instances. The officials are the only ones who can stop the action for any of the following reasons:

➢ If a player breaks a rule and receives a penalty.

- If the goalie stops a shot and holds onto the puck.
- If the puck goes out-of-play by flying out of the rink.
- If the referee determines if a player is seriously injured.
- If the goal cage is dislodged and moves off its spot.
- If a player is injured and his team has possession of the puck.
- If a player catches the puck in his/her hand and it's declared dead.
- If the referee loses sight of the puck in a crowd of players.
- If the puck cannot be moved after being stuck underneath a player or between a player's stick or skate and the boards; the puck is said to be frozen.

Each team is allowed one time out per period, but it must be called when the play has already been stopped for any of the above reasons.

Chapter 5 - The Play

A hockey game is played in 3 equal periods. Below the Squirt level the periods are 16 minutes with a running clock, which means it does not stop during play. The Squirt level plays with a running clock only in the third period. The first and second periods have a clock that does stop for the reasons listed in the previous chapter. From peewee up through high school the periods are 15 minutes long with a regular clock, meaning it is stopped for reasons listed in the previous chapter

Face-off - All ice hockey games begin with a face-off in the center face-off circle. This action is also used to start the second and the third periods, and after a score.

Face Off

A face-off is the chosen method of seeing that both teams have an equal opportunity of gaining possession of the puck to start play. Two opposing players, usually the centers, take a position in the face-off circle, facing each other and the opponent's goal, with their sticks touching the ice. The referee drops the puck between the two sticks and each player scrambles to gain control of the puck, or passes it to a teammate. The other players, except the goalie, must line up at locations outside the 30 foot diameter center face-off circle. The respective goalies position themselves in front of the goal they are defending.

The team whose player wins the face-off is immediately on offense while the other team is immediately on defense and the continuous action is in full swing. Stoppage of play only happens when one of the 9 circumstances in the previous chapter takes place, and at the end of the first, and second periods.

After the face-off the continuous action begins and the activity begins in earnest. In the course of just a few minutes your team may play offense, and switch to defense, several times. Be aware of which they do the most; are they constantly in their own zone defending, or are they in the attacking zone most of the time. The first one is bad, and the second one is good.

Penalties – there are team penalties, and there are individual penalties. All penalties are the result of violating a rule, called an infraction. Some are considered minor, and some are considered major:

> The three most common team penalties are offside, two-line pass, and icing. Team penalties result in a face-off:
> *Offside* – the rule says all attacking players must follow the puck over the attacking zone blue line; they must not go in ahead of the puck. The resulting face-off is outside the attacking zone nearest the place where the offside occurred.
> *Two-line pass* – this occurs when a player passes the puck from his/her defending zone to a teammate and it crosses the blue line and the red center line. The face-off is held at the point from which the illegal pass was made.
> *Icing* – this infraction comes when an offensive player shoots the puck from behind the red line to the other end with the purpose of stalling, or delaying the game. The face-off is held nearest to where the offending player shot the puck.

There are several individual penalties that can remove a offending player from the game and require him/her to serve playing time in the penalty box. In this case the offending player's team must play with one less player, which puts them at a disadvantage and they attempt to *kill the penalty,* which means they defend their goal not allowing a score until the penalty time runs out. The team with a 1 player advantage is on a *power play* and positions their players at locations where they can take advantage of having more players. It is possible for a team to have more than 1 player in the penalty box at the same time. That is a very bad thing.

Individual penalties can be either minor, or major. The time spent in the penalty box for a minor penalty is 2 minutes, and for a major penalty it's 5 minutes. Minor penalties are called for:
- Interference
- Tripping
- Boarding
- Cross-checking
- Slashing
- Charging
- Elbowing
- Holding
- High-sticking
- Hooking
- Playing with a broken stick
- Deliberately falling on the puck
- Holding the puck against the boards
- Leaving the bench illegally
- Roughing
- Some equipment violations

A player may be assessed a *double minor* for an accidental infraction that results in injury, or for an attempt to injure a player without actually causing an injury. The time in the penalty box for a double minor is 4 minutes.

Major penalties are assessed for the minor infractions listed above when the referee judges the action to be a greater degree of ferocity or deliberate ferocity was used. A minor penalty infraction that draws blood is an automatic major. Fighting, spearing, butt-ending, checking from behind, and clipping are also majors.

There are other types of penalties that are uncommon and rarely appear. They include misconduct through improper language, throwing something on the ice from the player bench, interfering with the game.

The following chapter on rules will provide sketches of the official's signal for the various infractions.

As the game has progressed over the decades so have the rules. Some interesting rule changes, and events, in the earlier days were:

1900 – the introduction of the first goal net
1912 – number of players on the ice reduced from 7 to 6.
1929 – the offside rule introduced
1937 – the first rule dealing with icing.
1949 – first use of the center red line
1955 – the Zamboni machine first used.

Wait a minute! Is that legal?

Chapter 6 – The Rules

The rules for hockey on the high school level are written and administered by the National Federation of State High School Associations (NFHS). Youth leagues and the younger programs play to high school rules, but make local adjustments, additions, or deletions. If you're in doubt, check with your league officials for clarification.

Before I get into the specifics of the rules I want to discuss *checking* or *cross checking*. These actions, which are a part of hockey, are not allowed in youth sports in age levels younger than 13 years old. Checking is the act of using any part of the body, or stick on an opposing player to knock them into the boards, or down on the ice. In the United States the ban on checking in youth hockey came in 2010, and it has also been banned in Canada. It is controversial and there are many advocates in favor of the younger players learning how to check, and defend against a check. The American Academy of Pediatrics study showed a higher incident of concussions in younger players resulting from checking.

A hockey game can be fast and furious and it is sometimes hard to follow that small puck. From a spectator point, you can't always see what is happening, or what just happened. In those cases you rely on the game officials signals to tell you.

The gestures and signals shown here are the official's way of communicating with the two teams, their coaches, and the spectators. The officials have a difficult job because they must exercise their best judgment, sometimes in a split second. They also must exert their authority in controlling a hockey game, making it run smoothly, and protecting the players.

Official's signals follow:

BOARDING – pounding a closed fist into the open palm of the opposite hand.

BUTT ENDING - crossing motions of the forearms – one passing over the other.

CHARGING – clenched fist rotating around each other in front of the chest.

CHECKING – arm movement from shoulder and extended in sweeping motion.

CLIPPING – tapping the leg.

CONTACT TO THE HEAD – tapping the top of the head.

CROSS CHECKING – when a player hold his/her stick in both hands and drives into an opposing player.

DELAY OF GAME – sweeping motion from chest to fully extended to the side.

DELAYED PENALTY – arm extended straight above the head.

ELBOWING – tapping the elbow with the opposite hand.

FIGHTING OR PUNCHING – double punching motion arms extended in front.

GOAL SCORE – a successful goal has been scored.

GRABBING OPPONENTS FACE MASK – simulate grabbing the mask.

HAND PASS – arm swung forward with open hand.

HIGH-STICKING – both hands clenched held one just above the other at forehead level.

HIT FROM BEHIND – arm placed behind the back with elbow bent.

HOLDING – Clasping one wrist with the other hand just in front of the chest.

HOLDING THE STICK – one hand grabs the other, and then arms extended with fists clenched.

HOOKING – tugging motion with both arms, as though pulling something toward him/her.

ICING – the back official will extend his arm at an angle, and then go to the face-off circle and fold his arms across his chest.

INTERFERENCE – fists closed with arms crossed and stationary in front of chest.

KNEEING – slapping the right palm to the left knee.

MISCONDUCT – both hands placed on the hips, then pointing to the penalized player.

OBSTRUCTION - hands in front of the body in the form of an O.

OFFSIDES – linesman points to the blue line.

PENALTY SHOT – arms crossed above head with fists clenched.

ROUGHING – a thrusting motion of the arm extending from the side.

SLASHING – a chopping motion with the edge of one hand on the opposite forearm.

SPEARING –stabbing motion with both hands in front of the body.

TIME-OUT – making a T with both hands.

TRIPPING – hitting right leg with right hand below the knee.

WASH-OUT – both arms swung laterally across the body with palms facing down to disallow a goal.

Chapter 7 – The Game

Okay, now it's time to play a game! Your player has been practicing hard and learning; you have read and absorbed all the information in this book – we are ready, so drop that puck.

A hockey game includes an abundance of strategic maneuvering by the opposing coaches. The offense is probing the defense for weaknesses trying to find what will be consistently successful. The opposing coach is doing exactly the same thing. There is a lot of guessing, anticipating, and searching on both sides, not to mention all of the constructive shouting from the spectators.

In order to reduce some of the guess work and help prepare for an upcoming opponent, coaches use a scheme called *scouting.* Scouting is legal and done openly, and is simply watching the upcoming opponent play another team so their tendencies can be noted. What do they like to do on offense? Who are their strongest players? Are they good skaters? What are their weaknesses? How do they play defense? What skill level is their goalie? What will work against them? A coach wants to know all the strengths and weaknesses of his/her next opponent.

There are a number of elements you could watch for in a hockey game so you can follow the progress, determine the trends, and understand what's happening. You will obviously be partial towards your team and want to be aware of its efforts, so here are a few factors for you to keep track of.

Always be aware of the ebb and flow. Remember this is a continuous action game and the switch from offense to defense can happen quickly. Is your team on offense a great deal of the time, or are they defending most of the time? Which team seems to have the faster skaters? Is your team getting shots on goal? Or is the other team out shooting your players? Are your players' abilities about the same as the opponent's players? Is one side obviously more advanced than the other? Is everyone working hard and giving strong efforts?

In all levels there are times when one team is superior to the other. It can be better players, more experienced players, better coaching, better attitudes, or something else, but one team gets walloped. Your team may be the wallopor, or the wallopee on that day.

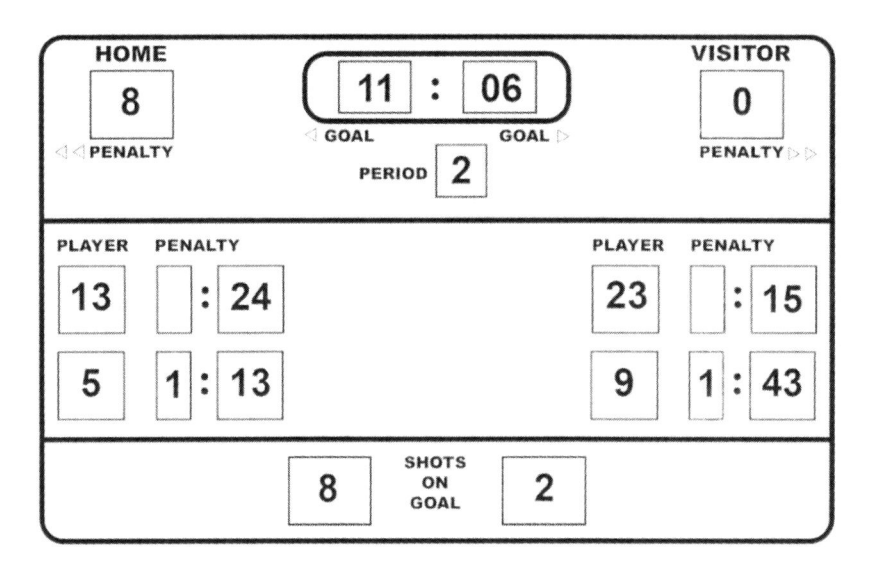

HOME			VISITOR
8	11 : 06		0
PENALTY	GOAL GOAL		PENALTY
	PERIOD 2		

PLAYER	PENALTY		PLAYER	PENALTY
13	: 24		23	: 15
5	1 : 13		9	1 : 43

SHOTS ON GOAL: 8   2

Both extremes need to be handled post game. It's no fun to get beaten badly, and it's of no value to beat the other team badly. In either case, they must be put into perspective. If your team gets beaten badly, there still should be encouragement for your player. Remind him/her that they are still good kids, playing hard, and doing the best they can. On any given day a person can have a bad day and there is no shame in that. If they tried, and worked hard, they were successful regardless of the final score. If your team should beat another team badly what are you going to say? I don't recommend you gloat, or celebrate and belittle the other players. Put it in perspective – congratulate your player, and his/her teammates. Remind them it's only one game, and to show sportsmanship.

Be aware of the official's role, and the meaning of their signals and gestures. As a spectator you cannot see everything that happens on the rink so you must rely on the officials to inform you. Being an official is a tough job and they can be the object of much scorn and criticism. Most do a fine job under tough circumstances. They are human beings and make occasional mistakes, or misjudgments. Give them credit for being an official and giving of their time so that kids can play games.

Watch the *puck* because it will always take you to the action. Each of these factors is practical in watching a hockey game. By being familiar with them you can determine what the trend of the game is and judge the relative success your team is having. However, there is one other little item that I highly recommend. *Watch your player*! If allowed in your area, put a little colored tape on their helmet so they are easier to spot, you can't always see their jersey number.

With the young, pre-high school players it is important for adults to be humble in winning and gracious in defeat. Losing a hockey game is not a failure, and players should not feel like it is. In sports, the best and longest lasting lessons come from not winning. It reveals what must be improved, or changed. You learn from defeat much more valid lessons than you do from winning. "If there is no struggle, there is no progress," Fredrick Douglas.

You're an expert on hockey now, and you know what position your player plays. You know his/her responsibilities on the rink. You know the objective of both the game and THE GAME. You know what your team is trying to accomplish, so you know what he/she is trying to contribute. You are aware of the physical skill and mental alertness it requires to participate in hockey. You are prepared to share in his/her elation and his/her despair because you have a more extensive knowledge of what he/she is doing. You are involved.

One last gentle warning and one last piece of advice. Remember it's just a game. It has the potential for grand life lessons, but it's just a game. Encourage and support your player and help to level out the highs and lows they will experience. However, don't misunderstand by diminishing the importance of doing a job well. Each player on a team has a specific, assigned job to do. They each need to do it with the best of their ability, with passion, and with purpose. Even though I say it's just a game, it should be a best effort every time. Help them accept their responsibility and to react with great physical and mental effort. If your player is struggling, talk to them and see if they understand their job. Sometimes a players' lack of effort is tied directly to confusion. If he/she is confused, help them to understand, and talk with the coach if necessary.

CONGRATULATIONS!
HAPPY HOCKEY!

Glossary

Assist – the pass that goes to the goal scorer immediately preceding the goal.

Attacking Zone – the area between the opponent's blue Line and their goal.

Blind Pass – passing the puck without looking.

Blue Lines – two wide blue colored lines that separate the rink into three zones. They are used to determine off sides and icing.

Boarding – a minor penalty when a player uses any method to throw an opponent into the boards.

Boards – the 4 foot wall that surrounds the rink.

Body Check – the act of bumping an opposing player with the hip or shoulder to knock him/her off balance. Only allowed against the player in possession of the puck, or the player who just passed the puck to a teammate.

Breakaway – when a player in possession of the puck skates towards the goalie after he/she has gotten clear of the defensive players.

Butt-ending – a major penalty resulting from a player jabbing an opponent with the shaft of his/her stick.

Center – the player lining up between the 2 forwards – takes part in most face-offs – leads the attack and controls his/her team's offense.

Center Face-off Circle – a 30 foot diameter circle located at the center of the rink. This circle is used for face-offs to start each period and after a goal has been made.

Center Ice – the area between the 2 blue lines, and also known as the neutral zone.

Center Line – the red line mid-way between the 2 goals running from to each side.

Charging – a minor penalty when a player takes a run at an opponent to body check.

Clearing the Puck – getting the puck out of one's own defending zone.

Clipping – tripping an opponent from behind or below the knees.

Contact to the Head – hitting an opponent in the head.

Crease Lines – the red semi-circular lines in front of the net.

Cross Checking – when a player holds his/her stick with both hands and drives into an opposing player.

Dead Puck – a puck that has gone out of play, or is held by a player.

Defending Zone – the area between the blue line and the goal being defended.

Delay of Game – a minor penalty on any player who intentionally delays the game.

Delayed Penalty – a delay in calling a penalty in order to let play continue.

Drop Pass – when a player simply leaves the puck behind for a teammate following him/her.

Elbowing – when a player strikes an opponent with his/her elbow to impede his/her progress.

Empty Net Goal – a goal scored against a team that has pulled its goalie.

Endboards – the boards (wall) at each end of the rink.

Fighting or Punching - act of hitting an opposing player with a open hand or fist.

Forward Line – consists of a right wing, a left wing, and the center.

Goal – when the puck is shot into the opponent's goal net – scores 1 point.

Hand Pass – when a player passes the puck to a teammate by hand.

Hat Trick – when a player scores 3 or more goals in a game.

High-Sticking – occurs when a player carries his/her stick above the normal height of the opponent's shoulders and hits or menaces the opponent with it.

Holding – when a player grabs and holds onto an opponent (or his/her) stick to impede their progress.

Hooking – when a player attempts to impede the progress of an opponent by hooking any part of the opponent's body with the blade of his/her stick.

Holding – grabbing an opponent or his/her stick.

Hooking – using the stick or blade to hinder an opponent from pursuing the puck.

Icing – when a player of the team in possession of the puck shoots it from behind the red center line across the opponent's goal line into the end of the rink and a member of the opponent's team touches it first.

Interference – when a player attempts to impede the progress of an opposing player not in possession of the puck.

Kneeing – when a player uses a knee to hit his/her opponent in the leg, thigh, or lower body.

Line Change – when the entire forward line is replaced.

Linesman – on-ice officials responsible for calling penalties and controlling the game.

Major Penalty – a penalty called for the more serious infractions – 5 minutes in the penalty box.

Misconduct – a misconduct penalty can be issued for many reasons – such as continuing to fight, disrespect to an official, using abusive language, throwing something on the ice from the player's bench, using racial slurs, etc. A misconduct could result in a 10 minute penalty and/or ejection.

Minor Penalty – a penalty for minor infractions – 3 minutes in the penalty box.

Net – the goal; netting attached to the frame of the uprights and crossbar.

Neutral Zone – the area at mid-ice between the 2 blue lines.

Obstruction – using the body, or stick to obstruct an opponent from pursuing the puck.

Offside – a violation that occurs when both skates of an attacking player crosses the opponents blue line ahead of the puck.

On the Fly – is making substitutions while play is under way.

Penalty Box – an area with a bench behind the sideboards where penalized players sit out their penalty time.

Power Play – an attack by a team against an opponent who is short a player, or players, because they are in the penalty box.

Redline – the line that divides the rink into 2 equal parts.

Referee – the chief official on the ice responsible for making sure the rink, ice, clock, and nets are in working order. The referee makes the final decision in any disputes. He/she starts the game with a face-off and calls penalties during the game.

Roughing – pushing or shoving altercation between players.

Save – the act of the goalie in blocking or stopping a shot on goal.

Seam – the gap between 2 or more defending players.

Shorthanded – a team with one or more players in the penalty box when the opposing team is at full strength.

Sideboards – the boards, or wall, along each side of the rink.

Slap Shot – a shot in which the player raises his/her stick in a backswing motion with his/her strong hand held low on the shaft and his/her other hand on the end as a pivot; when the stick comes down the player leans into the stick to put all his/her power into the shot.

Slashing – when a player swings his/her stick hard at an opponent, whether they make contact or not.

Slot – the area immediately in front of the goal.

Spearing – occurs when a player jabs, or attempts to jab the point of his stick into an opposing player's body.

Stick Handling – moving the puck along the ice with the stick blade.

Tripping – When a player uses his/her stick, or body under or around the feet or legs of an opponent causing them to lose their balance.

Wash Out – signal that a goal try was unsuccessful.

Wings – the two players that flank the center on his/her right and left sides.

Wrist Shot – a shot made using a strong flicking of the wrist and foreman.

Zamboni – the brand of machine used to clean or flood the ice before the game and between periods.

One Last Thing

Just one more thing before you leave. Please review and comment on this book. Good bad or indifferent – it's important. Go back to the site where you bought the book, put the title in the search box – when it comes up you'll see a link to review.

Thank you,
R. Benjamin Jordan (a.k.a. Coach Grampa)

Other sports books by R. Benjamin Jordan
    Origins and Evolution of American Football
    Football Just For Moms – And Anyone Else That's Interested
    Soccer Just for Moms – And Anyone Else That's Interested

More sports books coming winter of 2016/2017
    Lacrosse Just for Moms – And Anyone Else That's Interested
    Volleyball For Moms – And Anyone Else That's Interested

Novellas by R. Benjamin Jordan (a.k.a. Coach grampa)
- **Jimmie and the Recluse**
  A boy dealing with the loss of his father in WWII and looking for answers
- **Charlie Bradford**
  A young policeman coping with a personal tragedy, and meaning to his life
- **Stumble and Sting**
  Two inept and unlikely characters hunting down bad guys

A reminder – check them out:
    www.YouthSportsPsychology.com
    www.KidsSportsPsychology.com
    www.usahockey.com

JUST ONE MORE THING

Before you leave, please review and comment on this book. Good, bad, or indifferent – it's important. Go back to the site where you bought the book put the title in the search box – when it comes up you'll see a link to review.

Thank you
R. Benjamin Jordan

Other sports books by R. Benjamin Jordan
- Origins and Evolution of American Football
- Football Just For Moms – And Anyone Else That's Interested
- Soccer Just for Moms – And Anyone Else That's Interested

More sports books coming winter of 2016/2017
- Lacrosse Just for Moms – And Anyone Else That's Interested
- Volleyball For Moms – And Anyone Else That's Interested

Novellas by R. Benjamin Jordan:

Jimmie and the Recluse
A boy dealing with the loss of his father in WWII and looking for answers

Charlie Bradford
A policeman coping with a personal tragedy, and meaning to his life

Stumble and Sting
Two inept and unlikely characters hunting down bad guys

A reminder – check out:
- www.YouthSportsPsychology.com
- www.KidsSportsPsychology.com
- www.usahockey.com